Introducing Screen Printing

Introducing Screen Printing

Anthony Kinsey

B T Batsford Limited   London

Watson-Guptill Publications   New York

© Anthony Kinsey 1967

Published 1967 by B T Batsford Limited
4 Fitzhardinge Street, London W1

Published 1968 by Watson-Guptill Publications
165 West 46th Street, New York, NY 10036

Library of Congress Catalog Card Number 68–10050

Printed and bound in Denmark by F E Bording Limited
Copenhagen and London

Contents

Acknowledgment	6
Introduction	7
A word to teachers	8
The basic principle	9
Basic equipment and materials	10
The screen frame	12
Squeegees	14
Paint, ink or dye	16
Commercial inks	19
Covering the screen frame	20
Masking	22
The arrangement of the printing area	24
Using the squeegee	26
A word of advice	28
Preliminary experiments	29
Other methods of blocking out the screen	33
Producing a 'positive' screen	36
Proprietary stencil techniques	38
Register	39
The production of textures	41
Producing screen photographically	42
Fabric printing	45
Posters	47
Posters and the teacher	48
General hints	49
Summary of experiments	50
'Negative' methods	50
'Positive' methods	53
Substances used in screen printing	56
Recipes	58
Examples of techniques	61
Bibliography	96

Acknowledgment

My thanks are due to many people for their help and encouragement in the production of this book. In particular to my students at Brentwood College of Education who, together with pupils at two London comprehensive schools, have been at the receiving end in screen printing classes where much of the experience contained in this book has been gained. My thanks are also due to the Society for Education Through Art who have provided me with additional opportunities to widen my experience of teaching the subject.

I owe a special debt of gratitude to my friend Robert Borchard of the Fine Art Department of Ohio University for much helpful advice and permission to reproduce three of his prints.

London 1967   **A K**

Introduction

The process discussed in this book is a method of printmaking generally referred to as silk screen printing, although the American term *serigraphy* is now widely used to describe the medium when referring to the production of artists' prints.

Basically, screen printing is a form of stencilling and has long been used as a commercial process of reproduction in advertising and allied printing industries, and in the production of high quality fabrics and wallpapers. In the hands of the artist it is an exciting and stimulating medium requiring very little in the way of specialised equipment and allowing great freedom for experiment and invention. For this reason it is beginning to play an important part in the creative work of schools and colleges.

The importance of technical considerations in the creation of a work of art is a subject that has always been keenly debated. There is no doubt however that the act of mastering a new medium, understanding its limitations, and exploring its possibilities, often provide the artist with a stimulus of a kind not provided by any other type of creative activity.

No book can possibly explain how to produce a work of art. The intention of this book is to introduce the reader to this exciting medium; to describe the materials and equipment required for its practice, and to suggest some experiments which will provide a basis of experience from which further work can proceed.

A word to teachers

There are fashions in education as there are in most human activities. Subjects increase and decrease in popularity, crafts come and go. It is possible to compose a substantial list of craft subjects which have come and gone only to return again in the fullness of time or when the wheel of educational fashion has turned full circle.

What the teacher looks for in a school craft is surely an activity which will provide the student with the greatest possible opportunity for creative expression; something that offers far more than just a training in a particular skill. What the student needs is an activity which will assist in the development of his understanding and appreciation of form, colour, design and texture. He requires to be placed in a creative situation to which he can contribute something of himself.

Screen printing is a craft that satisfies most of these educational requirements whilst being at the same time reasonably easy to establish in the school situation. The craft is rapidly becoming popular, particularly in modern secondary schools, and there is no doubt that taught sympathetically, screen printing does provide an invaluable experience for the student at a level which allows him to experiment and make discoveries for himself.

The basic principle

A printing screen consists simply of a rectangular frame over which some loosely woven material (silk or cotton organdie) is stretched, making what is in effect a very fine sieve. The material is 'blocked out' wherever the designer requires the image to remain white or unprinted, and colouring matter is then brushed or squeegeed through the mesh of the material. In other words screen printing is simply a form of stencilling with the warp and weft of the material holding the pieces of stencil in place, thereby avoiding the need for 'tie bars'. Also the designer is not restricted to cutting his stencil in paper. Almost any substance which can be painted or stuck on to the material and which will not dissolve or become detached in the printing medium will serve as a blocking out agent, provided, of course, that whatever is used does not add appreciably to the thickness of the material and obstruct the squeegee.

In common with most printing techniques it is possible to develop screen printing to a very sophisticated level employing photographic and other processess, some of which will be touched upon in this book; but the basic principle is so simple that the printer needs very little experience of the medium before he can begin to invent and develop techniques for himself.

1a   A letter 'O' in a conventional stencil showing 'tie bars' holding the centre in place

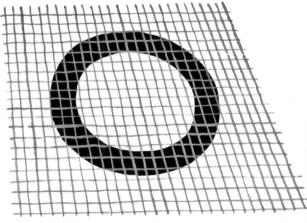

b   A screen printed 'O' showing the mesh of the material holding the centre in place

Basic equipment and materials

There are really only two special items of equipment used in screen printing: the screen itself and the squeegee. All the other equipment is of the kind generally found in the classroom or studio.

It is useful to have a sink and a source of water in the room where the printing is to be done, but it is possible to manage with a large plastic washing-up bowl, so long as it can be emptied and refilled fairly easily. If equipping a studio or classroom especially for the craft, a rare luxury, it is advantageous to have a rectangular sink unit installed size enough to accommodate the largest screen likely to be used. It is also, of course, a considerable advantage to have a piped supply of hot water. A gas or electric point, from which a heating ring or plate can be run, is desirable although a camping stove is adequate.

For printmaking, a special printing table is not necessary and any flat-topped table will do, but for fabric printing, other than on a very small scale, it is essential to have a properly prepared printing surface, one to which the fabric can be fixed before printing. A good printing table can be made easily by covering one side of a sheet of blockboard or chipboard with a layer or two of blanket followed by a sheet of waterproof cloth or plastic; the kind of waterproof plastic used in the building trade is very good for this purpose. Each layer can be stretched tight and tacked down to the other side of the board.

In this way a satisfactory printing surface can be provided quite cheaply. This portable printing surface would be supported on an ordinary table and when not in use put away with the covered side leaning against a wall.

2   The basic equipment required to begin the preliminary experiments in screen printing

Screen	Jam jars	Cream and Yoghurt cartons
Squeegee	Rags	
Clean newspaper	Sponge	Adhesive tape or gumstrip
Spoon	Scissors	
Flat iron	Coffee tins	Drawing pins (thumb tacks) or a staple gun
Bowl	Paint brushes	

The screen frame

The screen consists of a simple rectangular frame made out of timber, soft enough to take drawing pins or staples, and yet firm enough to withstand the considerable stresses put on it by stretching the covering material. Old picture frames can be used but they are not generally satisfactory. All too often they are made from oak or some other hardwood into which it is almost impossible to press the drawing pins (thumb tacks) when stretching the organdie. Also picture frames generally have a rebate or some other form of moulding that makes cleaning difficult.

Professionally-made screen frames are obtainable from specialist suppliers and ideally are made of rot-proof cedarwood. The economy of screen printing, one of its main features, is due however to the fact that most of the necessary equipment can be made quite easily in the home or school. There are several methods of constructing a screen, the choice depending on the degree of carpentry skill available. For sizes up to about 2 ft by 1½ ft, ordinary 2 in. by 1 in. softwood is the most useful and can be purchased readily from a local timber (lumber) supplier or 'hobby' shop. Jointing the corners is not really difficult and the simplest joints are satisfactory for this purpose provided that oval nails, which can be hammered home without splitting the wood, and a reliable waterproof glue are used. As when making a picture frame the whole construction is only truly rigid when the final joint has been put together, so do not despair if the first couple of joints seem to be a little weak when assembled. Narrow corrugated fasteners are very useful for pulling the corners together, but hammering them into place does require some skill and experience.

It is advisable to make all the screens the same size in the first instance so that you can be sure that your squeegees will fit them all. It is also a good plan to relate the size of your screens to the width of the covering material that you intend to use as, for the sake of economy, you will want to avoid cutting the material to waste.

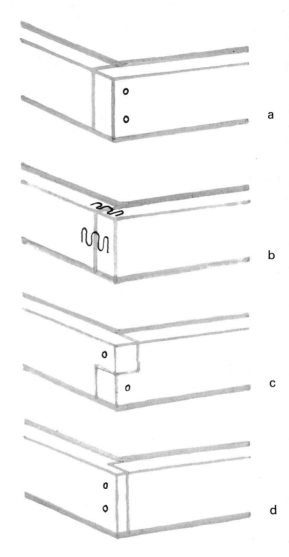

3 A basic wooden screen frame and four methods
of jointing the corners
a A simple butt joint glued and pinned with oval
   nails
b The same joint this time fixed with corrugated
   dogs
c A simple halving joint glued and pinned
d A shoulder joint glued and pinned

Squeegees

The colouring matter in which the design is to be printed can be brushed through the screen with a wide decorator's brush, but the most useful and efficient implement for this purpose is a squeegee, consisting of a flat blade of rubber supported by a wooden handle. Like screens, squeegees can easily be made in the classroom or studio and can vary in complexity according to the maker's ability with a hammer and saw. The most simple consists of nothing more than a strip of rubber fixed with large-headed galvanised or copper nails to a length of wood, possibly a piece of 2 in. by 1 in. timber left over from making a screen. The rubber strip is best obtained from a specialist supplier although it is possible to make do with substitute material such as draught-excluder; even a strip of hardboard can be used provided that the edge is really straight and has been carefully sanded down. However, there is no real substitute for the correct material which is sold by the foot as 'squeegee rubber' in a number of widths and thicknesses. Generally the 2 in. by $\frac{1}{4}$ in. strip is the best for the kind of work suggested in this book.

Some commercially-produced squeegees have the working edge of the rubber cut to a 'V' section like the blade of a knife. I can see no great advantage in this and, as shaping rubber with any accuracy is a difficult process, I would recommend that the beginner leaves his rubber blade with a square section, as this is much more likely to remain true during the period of use.

An additional refinement to the squeegees illustrated is a strip of wood fixed along the back of the handle long enough to overhang the sides of the screen frame. This device prevents the handle of the squeegee slipping into the pigment in the screen, and allows the operator to leave the squeegee in the screen throughout the printing process.

The length of the squeegee blade should be about $1\frac{1}{2}$ in. shorter than the inside width of the screen frame to permit easy movement backwards and forwards.

14

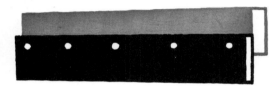

4   Methods of making a squeegee

a   The rubber is simply nailed to the side of a wooden strip

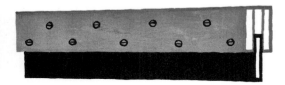

b   The rubber is sandwiched between two wooden strips with another strip of wood of exactly the same thickness as the rubber filling the empty space

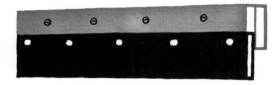

c   The rubber and a strip of wood of the same thickness are fixed to one side of a larger wooden strip

d   The rubber is set in a strip of wood that has been ploughed to take it

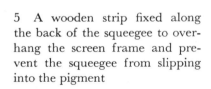

5   A wooden strip fixed along the back of the squeegee to overhang the screen frame and prevent the squeegee from slipping into the pigment

Paint, ink or dye

In practice, almost any kind of pigment and base can be used with a screen provided that:

(a) it is of the correct consistency, i. e. not so thin that it will spread or run under the blocked out sections of the screen, or so thick that it will not pass through the mesh of the organdie;

(b) that it will not dry so quickly that the screen cannot be left for a moment or two without blocking up.

In general terms there are three kinds of colouring matter, (1) paint, (2) ink, (3) dye. Although this is not a scientific form for classification, it will serve our purpose. Under the first heading we can include the kind of improvised material not strictly designed for screen printing but which is normally available in a studio or classroom. For early experimental work on paper, probably the simplest pigment to use is ordinary tempera powder paint. This should be mixed with water to a paste consistency, and just before printing a little glycerine can be added to provide extra body, and at the same time prevent the pigment and water separating under the pressure of the squeegee. Care must be taken to ensure that there are no lumps of unmixed pigment in the paint as these would cause streaks on the print. This is something that has to be guarded against when mixing any medium for use with screen printing. Poster paint, diluted slightly with water, can also be used for screen printing but would probably tend to be rather expensive if used extensively.

One major disadvantage of paint as a medium of screen printing is its opacity, as this does not permit the very exciting overprint effects which are potentially such a feature of this printing technique.

The use of the word 'dye' in connection with screen printing automatically suggests printing on fabric. In fact many of the dyes produced for fabric printing, work equally well when used for printing on paper and, being transparent, do allow a wide range of overprinting effects. However, before going on to discuss commercially-produced dyes I would like to suggest a home-made mixture which works well, is inexpensive and easy to obtain. This is produced by adding domestic dye powder, the kind that can be obtained in small packets from most hardware stores, to any cellulose wallpaper paste. The latter should be mixed a little more thickly than is recommended by the manufacturer and as much dye added as is needed to produce the required colour. It is advisable to dissolve the dye powder in a little hot water before adding it to the paste. The coloured ink powders often supplied to schools work equally well and starch paste (wheat paste) can be used as an alternative to the cellulose. The one major disadvantage of this medium for work in schools is of course that it is a stain and as such is not always easy to remove from hands and clothing. Otherwise its cheapness and its transparency make it an excellent medium for preliminary work both on paper and on fabric. It must be realised however that as a dye, used in this form, it is not fast enough to be of any use for serious fabric printing where permanence and washability are required.

In recent years there have been many developments in the field of dyestuff production, particularly of oil-in-water emulsion dyes suitable for use with screens. Undoubtedly the next few years will see even more developments as new synthetic materials become available. The tendency has always been, and will always be, for the processes to become more and more simplified.

Many manufacturers of dyes are understandably reluctant to disclose the exact chemical composition of their products. Even those who supply what appear to be fairly complete formula usually include at least one basic 'mystery' ingredient which is given no exact chemical specification. I use proprietary names, therefore, in the certain knowledge that other screen printers will have preferences for other, similar, products manufactured by rival companies.

The cost of equipping a studio with a variety of different dyes is quite considerable so I have always made it a rule to find something good and stick to it. It takes time and effort to become conversant with the characteristics and possibilities of a particular medium, and on the whole, I feel that one stands to lose rather than gain from constantly changing from one brand of dyestuff to another.

The particular brand of dyestuff that I have chosen to refer to throughout this book, namely *Helizarin,* is the one that I have used extensively in my own work as a teacher and it has always proved reliable and easy to use both on fabric and on paper. Helizarin is a British product and for American readers I would suggest *Acco-Lite* as an equivalent product. I have however included the names of manufacturers of other, similar, products in the list of suppliers at the end of the book and I hope the reader will understand that it is only my familiarity with a particular medium that leads me to describe it rather than any other similar product.

Helizarin, in common with the other emulsion dyes, is not really a true dye in the strict sense of the word. Its penetration of the fabric on which it is printed is not complete and it is in practice something between a dye and a fabric ink. But for the purpose of printmaking on paper this is an advantage.

The recipe for mixing Helizarin, as supplied by the manufacturer, looks complicated but for printmaking on paper a simple mixture of the base, or binder, with some of the pigment is quite fast and durable. The pigment is very highly concentrated and is added drop by drop to the binder until the desired colour is achieved. Of course if the printer wishes to be in the position to be able to mix exactly the same shade a second time it is necessary to measure the quantities exactly.

None of these emulsion dyes is cheap and some economy is necessary in their use. Always keep the mixed dye in screw-topped jars for example, and do not mix up more dye than is needed for a particular printing session at one time. But for quality of print and ease of handling, emulsion dyes, such as Helizarin, possess many advantages for the beginner over most other media. One of their great virtues is that all screens and utensils can be washed in cold water. Technically any *fabric* printed with emulsion based dyes should be fixed on completion by heating it to a temperature of about 100-150°C for a specified period. In practice this means ironing it on both sides with a hot iron. Prints made on paper do not seem to need any treatment of this kind and I have hanging on my wall as I write, a screen print made at least ten years ago using Helizarin dye which, as far as I can judge, has lost none of its original freshness.

The question does arise as to the toxic nature of some of the materials used for screen printing particularly when teaching very young children. I think it would be rash to claim that emulsion based dyes were completely non-toxic and some discretion must be used. Most manufacturers of these dyes maintain that there is only a likelihood of danger when the substances are actually consumed in considerable quantities.

18

Commercial inks

Commercially-produced screen printing inks are almost invariably oil based and require the use of white spirit as a diluent during printing, and when cleaning screens and utensils. This is one of the main factors reducing the suitability of ink of this kind as a printing medium for use in large classes or with young children. Screen inks are also more expensive, volume for volume, than fabric dyes and to this cost must be added the cost of the cleaning spirit.

Although, on balance, I do not recommend the use of ink to the beginner for his early experiments, I would suggest that when he feels reasonably confident in his handling of a screen, and when printing conditions are suitable, he gives it a try.

Most screen inks are supplied in opaque form by the manufacturer; that is, one printed colour will completely cover another without the first colour showing through. To achieve the kind of overprinting obtained with emulsion fabric dyes it is necessary to use an additional substance usually referred to as 'reducing medium'. Reducing medium resembles thin honey in appearance and is used rather in the same way as the binder is used in the Helizarin process. A quantity of reducing medium is put into a receptacle (an empty tin or glass jar, *not* a plastic pot) and ink is added until the desired strength of colour has been obtained. It is usually necessary to add a little white spirit to the mixture just before printing to assist the flow through the screen.

All colours are completely intermixable and some very rich effects can be obtained using inks in this way. Print drying time is rather longer than that for fabric dye, and under no circumstances should a second print be attempted on the same sheet until the first colour is thoroughly dry.

Covering the screen frame

The traditional material for covering screen frames is silk. And silk, together with certain modern man-made fibres is still used extensively for commercial screen printing where durability and extremely fine and accurate work are required. For educational purposes, and for the kind of experimental work suggested in this book, silk is generally regarded as being far too expensive. The usual substitute is cotton organdie. This can be obtained from screen printing suppliers and also from most department stores. If the latter source of supply is used it would be advisable to experiment with a small quantity in the first instance to be sure that the weave of the cotton is open enough to allow the passage of the colouring matter as dressmaker's organdies tend to vary in this respect.

Covering the screen with organdie does present a few difficulties to the beginner, chiefly because the organdie has a way of tearing dramatically and without warning whilst it is being stretched.

After a little experience it is easy to gauge exactly how much tension the organdie will stand.

Although every effort should be made to stretch the organdie drum tight, any slack areas that remain after the beginner's first few attempts at stretching a screen should shrink out when the organdie becomes wet.

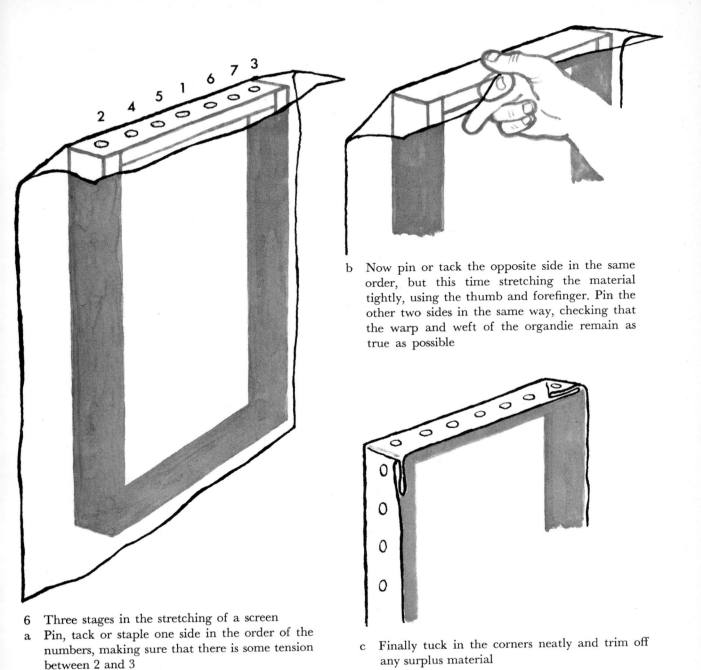

b Now pin or tack the opposite side in the same order, but this time stretching the material tightly, using the thumb and forefinger. Pin the other two sides in the same way, checking that the warp and weft of the organdie remain as true as possible

6 Three stages in the stretching of a screen

a Pin, tack or staple one side in the order of the numbers, making sure that there is some tension between 2 and 3

c Finally tuck in the corners neatly and trim off any surplus material

Masking

Before the screen can be used for printing it will have to be masked so that only a rectangle of organdie the size and shape of the design to be printed will remain open in the centre. The masked border thus formed will not only serve to control the overall dimensions of the printed design but will also act as a containing reservoir for the colour. One of the most usual ways of making this margin is to use 2 in. wide paper gumstrip which is stuck firmly to the organdie. Two strips should be used at each of the four sides, each pair overlapping by about ½ in. Care should be taken to ensure that the outside strips are brought well up the outside of the frame to stop any of the colour seeping out and spoiling the work. The secret of getting the gumstrip well and truly stuck down is to make sure it is thoroughly soaked first. A wringing wet sponge trailed along the strip or even running the strip under the tap or through a bucket of water is not too extreme. It is quite a good idea to cut all the strips to length before beginning the masking process. The roll of gumstrip can then be kept well out of the way of the water, as there is nothing more irritating than to find that the roll has been put down in a pool of water and has subsequently dried into a solid mass.

Many screen printers advocate sealing the inside as well as the outside of the screen. Whilst this might be necessary when preparing a screen for commercial use or for the production of many yards of fabric, I have always found that for most purposes it is quite sufficient to seal the outside only. In fact the less one has inside the screen to interfere with the passage of the squeegee the better.

In theory the constant contact of the gumstrip mask with water, either the water contained in the dye or the water used for washing out the screen after printing, should loosen the gum and cause the strip to fall away from the screen. In practice this rarely seems to happen, unless an excessive amount of water is used. More often that not the dye or ink builds up behind the gumstrip so that even when the gumstrip is removed that area of the screen remains blocked.

There are certain screen making techniques that do not require the preliminary application of a gumstrip border. These techniques are described on pages 33–38.

CHECKOUT SLIP
BROWN MEMORIAL LIBRARY

PHONE: 937-962-2377

Date charged: 10/30/2014,
19:27
Title: Introducing screen
printing
Item ID: 31705001129789
Date due: 11/20/2014,23:
59

Date charged: 10/30/2014,
19:27
Title: Screen printing :
design & technique
Item ID: 34294001380574
Date due: 11/20/2014,23:
59

brownmemorial.lib.oh.us

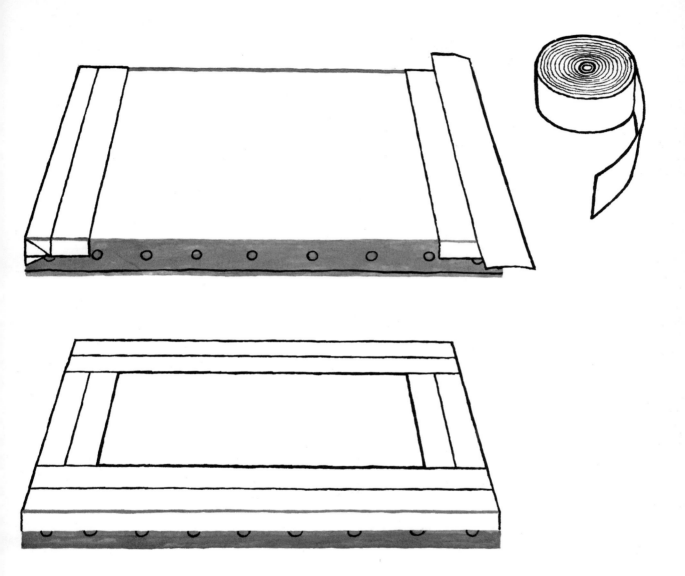

7 Gumstrip is stuck to the outside of the screen to form a mask to contain the pigment and at the same time control the size and shape of the print

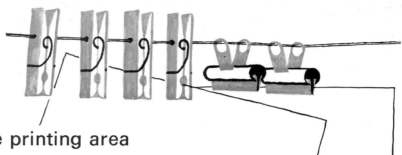

The arrangement of the printing area

The arrangement of the printing area is very important. The printer can soon find himself with a screen full of wet dye in his hands and surrounded by wet prints with nowhere to put anything down. A table arrangement, similar to the one illustrated, is usually satisfactory. It is also a great help to be able to rig up a simple device from which the prints can be suspended whilst they are drying. The various items of apparatus used for drying clothes can nearly always be adapted by means of 'bulldog' clips or even clothes pegs to accommodate any number of prints in a relatively confined space. Clothes pegs (clothes pins with coiled springs), for example, can be drilled and threaded on a string slung across the room.

We shall assume that for the first experiments a proper printing table is not available and that the printing surface is a table top on which there is a pad of newspaper. The area of this pad should be large enough to take the whole of the screen, and it is advisable to take some care when arranging the newspapers so that the pad is flat and even. The use of newspaper as a printing surface has one major advantage over the conventional printing table in that, should the top paper become stained and sticky with pigment, it can be removed and thrown away revealing a fresh sheet for the next print.

This gets round the problem of having to 'wipe down' repeatedly during the printing session. When using this system with a class, the problem of disposing of the old newspaper arises, and I found myself in the position more than once of having a lecture room almost half full of crumpled newsprint; a situation most unpopular with the caretaker. When arranging the printing area do not forget to allow space on the table for the screen when it is not in use, and a space for the squeegee should it be necessary to remove it from the screen during the course of the printing. When putting the screen down between prints it is a good idea to support one end with a strip of wood about 1 in. thick. This prevents the wet organdie from sticking to the table top and also, by tilting the screen, confines the pigment to one end.

Opposite

9 Clothes pegs (pins) or bulldog clips can be strung on a line to hold the wet prints. In the case of wooden clothes pegs a small hole will have to be drilled in each one as shown

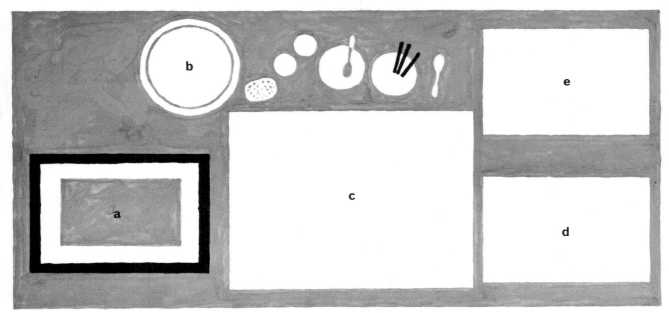

8   A satisfactory arrangement of the printing area

    a screen
    b bowl of water
    c printing surface
      (newspaper)
    d prints
    e printing paper

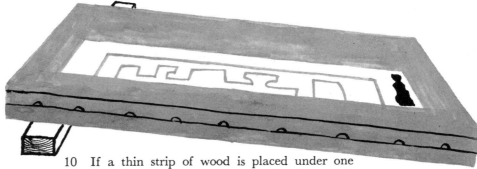

10   If a thin strip of wood is placed under one end of the screen between prints the pigment is confined to one end and the wet organdie is prevented from sticking to the table

Using the squeegee

The use of the squeegee for forcing the pigment through the mesh of the organdie is really one of the most difficult techniques for the beginner to master, and a little practice with a plain screen and water is well worth while before commencing the printing proper. The first problem is how to get an even spread of pigment along the right hand masking strip. If the pigment is dribbled from a jug or can, care must be taken to ensure that there is not an excessive amount of pigment at the beginning and end of the movement. The screen is then placed on the surface to be printed and held firmly in position. Finally with the rubber blade of the squeegee well to the right, behind the line of pigment, the colour is swept across the screen with a confident movement of the right hand. The free hand should be used to press the screen down firmly against the printing surface as under no circumstances should the screen be permitted to move during the printing process.

It is very useful to have an assistant at this stage, and when working with children or students I always encourage them to work in pairs, so that one of them is always available to hold the screen in position. This arrangement also has the advantage of halving the amount of space and equipment required during the experimental period of any screen printing course. It is very important not to hurry the squeegee across the screen. The movement should be firm and steady, never permitting any of the pigment to slip under the blade of the squeegee. When using transparent pigment, each movement of the squeegee across the face of the screen intensifies the tone of the print until eventually the printed surface becomes thoroughly soaked with pigment and will therefore accept no more.

It is normal procedure to use one forward and one backward movement of the squeegee to complete each print, ending up with the squeegee in position to commence the next print.

In whichever direction the squeegee is moving across the screen, the angle at which it is held should be the same, i. e. about 45°, with the top of the squeegee in advance of the blade. Care must be taken to ensure that there is a good ridge of colour in front of the rubber blade for both the backward and forward movements. This is particularly important when printing with transparent medium as it is quite impossible to correct the print if the colour should run out in the middle of a stroke.

11 The pigment should be spread as evenly as possible along the right hand masking strip. The amount of pigment required for a particular print will depend on the openness of the screen and the absorbency of the paper

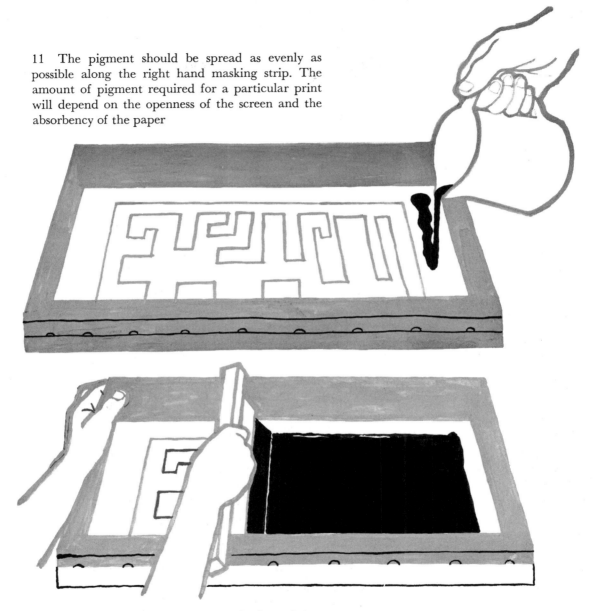

12 Squeegeeing the pigment across the face of the screen, one hand holding the screen in place, the other operating the squeegee at an angle of about 45°

A word of advice

We have discussed the basic equipment and procedure used in screen printing but much of what I have tried to explain, particularly some of the tips and cautions, will only really make sense when you have had the opportunity of actually duing some printing.

By working on the following exercises or experiments, practical experience of a few of the more fundamental techniques of screen printing will be gained. I will make no attempt to deal directly with the question of designing for screen printing as the problems of aesthetics have no place in a book of this kind which is concerned with the practical aspects of the subject. I do feel, however, that it is a mistake for the beginner to concern himself with any attempt at direct representational picture making, certainly in his first experiments, if at all.

I firmly believe that it is better to design *through* the medium than *for* the medium, and suggest that in the early experiments the reader works directly on to the screen, having very few preconceived ideas about the final results to be achieved. One of the fascinations of screen printing is the wide range of effects that one comes upon quite accidently and which can later be exploited in a more controlled fashion.

Preliminary experiments

In theory a screen is covered and prepared for one particular design or part of a design and when that printing is complete the organdie is stripped off the frame and the screen is re-covered. This of course is uneconomic for the beginner both in the use of organdie and in the time taken to re-prepare the screen. However, it is quite easy to devise techniques which permit the same screen covering to be used several times to print different designs. It is with this in mind that the experiments suggested in this section of the book are planned.

Any material or substance which will prevent the pigment from passing through the organdie without at the same time getting in the way of the squeegee can be used as a blocking out agent. Probably the easiest one to experiment with in the first instance is newsprint. Ordinary printed newspaper will do, but to achieve really clean prints it is much better if one can use plain newsprint (infant's brushwork paper), light coloured sugar or construction paper, or white lining paper. It is a mistake to use better quality paper for the purpose of blocking out the screen, for example, cartridge (drawing) paper, as it absorbs water rather slowly and will stretch and wrinkle whilst the screen is in use, allowing the pigment to seep through.

Cut some printing paper to the size most suitable for the screen you intend to use. It will probably be most convenient to cut the paper to something approaching the outside dimensions of the screen. Place a sheet of this paper in the centre of the printing pad and locate the screen over it. The effective printing area can be marked through the, as yet, completely plain screen with a soft pencil or a piece of charcoal. Remove the screen leaving the area to be printed marked on the printing paper. Some pieces of newsprint can now be torn or cut up and arranged to make a design to fill this area. None of these shapes should be larger than about a quarter of the total area or smaller than about 1 in. square. The screen can now be re-placed over the arrangement so that it shows through the organdie using the masked off area as a kind of window.

The pigment which should have been mixed to a fairly strong colour (but of a light enough tone to allow some scope for overprinting) should now be poured into the screen. This is then squeegeed across the screen making sure that the screen is held firmly in place. When the screen is removed it will be found that the pieces of paper making up the design have stuck to the underside of the organdie and that the printing paper remains white or unprinted where paper shapes have been. The screen can be used for many subsequent prints with the pieces of newsprint held in place by nothing more than the pigment used for the printing. When a particular sequence of prints is complete the newsprint can be removed with the aid of a wet sponge and the screen used again for a fresh design.

It is a good plan to make several, say half a dozen, prints of the first arrangement and before removing the pieces to re-print with the same colour, simply turning the screen round on itself. In this way one can have a good idea of the possibilities of the medium and the kind of overprinting effects that can be obtained. Interesting designs can be developed by printing the same screen several times on the same piece of printing paper whilst progressively adding new shapes to the screen or removing existing ones. Although relying solely on the pigment to hold the shapes to the screen it is remarkable how long such a screen will last. Eventually, however, the newsprint does become too saturated and weak to remain in position and a fresh start has to be made. A more controlled and permanent effect can be produced by cutting the shapes in gum-strip and sticking them directly into position on the underside of the organdie.

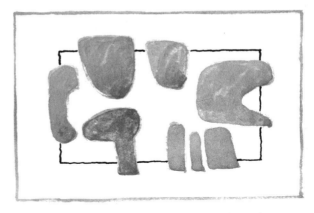

13a Marking the perimeter of the shape to be printed through the organdie with a soft pencil or charcoal

b Cut-out newsprint shapes placed on the marked sheet ready to be picked up by the screen

c Squeegeeing the pigment across the screen to pick up the newsprint shapes

d The printed design remaining when the screen has been lifted away

And when putting on the masking strips it is important to make sure that the gumstrip is well and truly soaked before it is pressed into place. When the time comes for the design to be changed the gumstrip can be removed by soaking it with water either in a sink or by using a wet sponge. There is a tendency, particularly when using dyes of the Helizarin type, for dye to set behind the paper used for blocking the screen so that when this is removed the organdie remains blocked with dye. In the event of this happening, which is usually only if the screen has been left unattended for long periods, the solid dye has to be removed with the aid of a special solvent supplied by the manufacturer. Modern paint strippers can be used to remove most dyes and paints should the correct solvent not be available.

There are many occasions when one wishes to change to a different colour during printing without dislodging the paper controlling the design, which would almost certainly happen if the screen were to be washed under a running tap. If the screen is placed on some sheets of newspaper, any unwanted pigment can be removed with a pallet knife (preferably square ended) or a spoon and the whole of the inside of the screen wiped out with a fairly dry sponge. Almost none of the original colour will remain and the paper pieces having been held in place against the newspaper will be ready for the next printing with the new colour. There are limits to this technique of course; it would be virtually impossible to clean out a black screen in this way and expect to be able to follow on with a printing in yellow or some other very pale colour.

Other methods of blocking out the screen

It is obvious that from the design point of view, although it possesses many fascinating possibilities, the technique of blocking out the screen with paper has its limitations. The designer is restricted to a design made up of shapes; it being almost impossible to produce lines and textures by this method. Designs of a more linear character can be produced by painting the organdie with almost any liquid which, when it is dry, will not break down in the particular medium used for printing; oil paint, lacquer, plastic emulsion paint, glue, some types of gum and paste, button polish (french polish or shellac), paraffin wax, are some of the most usual. Paraffin wax is particulary useful as, unlike most of the other media, it dries or rather sets almost at once, so that the screen is immediately ready for use. It is also very easy to remove from the organdie when a change of design is required, which is not the case with some of the other blocking out substances. Paraffin wax (the kind used for making candles) is, under normal temperature conditions, a solid substance and has to be melted down before it can be used. The usual method of doing this is to heat the wax in a water jacket, i. e. a glue pot, or failing that a tin can inside a saucepan of water; when liquid it can be painted on to the organdie with a paint brush or it can be splashed, dribbled or splattered to produce interesting textural effects. Some speed has to be used when applying the wax as it sets very quickly once it has been removed from the heated pan. Wax candles can be melted down to provide the liquid wax but it is really cheaper and more satisfactory to buy the wax by the pound in block form from a chemist or drug store. In this form it is free from impurities and has a low specified melting point, usually around 100° F. Care must be taken when applying the wax to ensure that it does not set into thick blobs or lines on the organdie, as these will obstruct the passage of the squeegee and give an uneven print. Any thick wax that does form in this way will have to be gently scraped away with a flat piece of wood, a wooden ruler for instance, while supporting the other side of the organdie with the palm of the hand. A screen prepared with wax will last for quite a large number of prints before breaking down. The wax is fairly soluble in spirit so that on the whole a wax prepared screen will have a much longer life when used with a water soluble ink or dye. Helizarin works very well with a wax screen.

14 Wax can be removed by ironing between pads of newspaper. If the wax is thick the newspaper should be changed, or at least turned round, from time to time

When the time comes for cleaning the screen, the wax can be removed by ironing the screen between sheets of newsprint with a warm iron, or by flooding the wax out by running the screen under a hot water tap to which a rubber extension, or a short length of hosepipe, has been attached. If the washing method is used it is important to rig up some kind of trap in the sink to prevent the wax from getting into the drainage system. Obviously the wax is not dissolved in the water and will only remain in a liquid state whilst the water is hot. The waste water will cool very quickly allowing the wax to solidify, causing a blockage in the drainage system.

Wax is a very suitable medium for developing or changing a design between printings. It is easy to add wax to the design before printing with the next colour; it is also possible to remove part of the wax by putting the screen down on a pad of newspaper and drawing into the wax with an ordinary electric soldering iron. Provided the iron is not permitted to remain in the same spot for too long the organdie will stand up to the heat, whilst the wax will melt and be absorbed into the newspaper pad.

All the other substances previously mentioned can be painted directly on to the screen. Many of them have an advantage over wax in that they are capable of reproducing much finer and more detailed work and have greater permanence. On the other hand their irremovability, together with the length of drying time required, makes most of these substances less suitable for early experiments. I would recommend experimenting for some time with the wax technique before going on to any of the other media.

15 Wax can be removed in a controlled way with an electric soldering iron

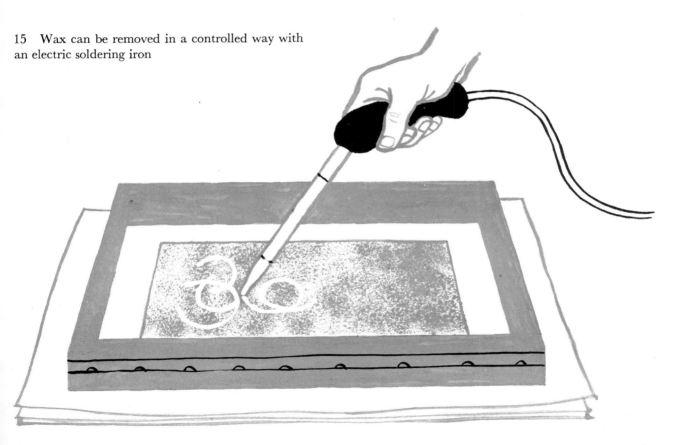

Producing a 'positive' screen

So far all the techniques suggested for producing a design on the screen have been of a 'negative' nature; that is to say, the work done on the organdie has resulted in white or unprinted areas on the printing paper. Obviously it is possible to reproduce a positive design by laboriously painting round the required shapes, rather in the way Victorian wood engravers reproduced pen drawings by cutting away the wood from each side of the line. This, however, is always a laboured, mechanical and inhibiting process. Fortunately there is a very simple and straightforward way of producing a positive screen. This consists of painting the design on to the organdie in paraffin wax, and then coating the whole screen with either a mixture of gelatine and potassium dichromate (see recipe page 58), or more simply with polyvinyl acetate (p.v.a. tempera colour medium, acrylic, or a white glue). Decorator's white emulsion paint can be used if it is more readily available. Once the coating is dry (emulsion paint or p.v.a. dries in about an hour in a warm room; gelatine and potassium dichromate takes very much longer and needs to be exposed to light for a time after it has dried) the wax, which has served to protect the organdie from the coating can be removed, leaving an open screen in its place. When printed this will produce a print identical with the original wax painting.

In essence this technique depends for its success on the use of two dissimilar substances, i.e. one which is water soluble, one which is either totally insoluble or soluble only in white spirit (mineral spirits) and petrol (gasoline) or alcohol, so that by using the appropriate solvent one of the substances can be removed without the other. Obviously there are many pairs of substances that could be used in this way, for example, black waterproofing compound of the kind used in the building trade (or asphaltum) which is soluble in white spirit (mineral spirits) or petrol (gasoline), and glue size which is soluble in water.

Gelatine and potassium dichromate when mixed together produce a photosensitive substance which can be very useful to the screen printer. The gelatine is dissolved in warm water in the same kind of water jacket as that used to melt the wax. The water should never be allowed to boil as this will affect the properties of the gelatine. When a little potassium dichromate is added to the gelatine a bright yellow substance is produced which remains soluble in water until it has dried and been exposed to light. The light has the effect of changing the colour to a dark gingery brown and making the gelatine completely insoluble in water.

It is possible to use gelatine and potassium dichromate to produce a screen photographically, see page 42.

Another technique for producing a 'positive' screen, which is in some ways similar to the one in wax, but which is considerably more controllable and capable of reproducing rather finer lines is a screen coated with *plain* gelatine. This is done by tilting the screen, bottom up, at an angle of about 45°, and, using a large soft brush, flooding the warm gelatine over the organdie, starting at the top and working systematically down, never letting the leading edge of the gelatine solidify. It may be necessary to repeat this process, preferably starting from the other end of the screen, to ensure that the mesh of the organdie becomes completely filled with gelatine. Drying time should be allowed between coats.

When the final coat is thoroughly dry the design can be painted on to the gelatine using lacquer. It is best to use specially prepared cellulose-based screen lacquer for this purpose, although ordinary japanese lacquer purchased from a hardware store works quite well if it is not too thin.

The lacquer must be painted on to the gelatine, i. e. on to the same side of the organdie as the gelatine is painted. In most cases this will be the bottom or outside of the screen, so it must be remembered that any design put on to the screen in this way will print as a mirror image.

The latter may not be a vital consideration when producing an abstract or non-figurative design but any such mistake when reproducing lettering would be disastrous. While the lacquer is drying, about a teaspoonful of potassium dichromate crystals should be dissolved in ¼ pint of water. This solution can then be painted very carefully over the top of the lacquer and gelatine. There will be a slight tendency for the potassium dichromate to soak into the gelatine and creep under the lacquer. This can be avoided if the potassium dichromate solution is applied sparingly and brushed-out thinly using a soft brush. The lacquer will have served to protect the gelatine from the potassium dichromate so that even after the screen has been allowed to dry and has been exposed to light the gelatine lying under the lacquer will still be soluble in warm water.

When the screen is washed in hot water the gelatine beneath the lacquer will dissolve taking the lacquer with it, and leaving an open screen in its place. A screen prepared in this way is very hard wearing and, if carefully cleaned between printing, will last indefinitely or at least until the organdie is accidentally damaged. This kind of screen needs no paper mask as the gelatine will perform that function, provided that the design has not been taken too close to the frame and that both the gelatine and the potassium dichromate have been painted well up the outside of the frame.

Proprietary stencil techniques

There are a number of proprietary film stencils on the market which, although chiefly intended for use by the commercial screen printer, are worth knowing about. These stencils are sold in the form of sheets which consist, basically, of a sheet of lacquer backed by a sheet of thin paper or plastic. Exact instructions for using these film stencils are supplied by the manufacturer but in general principle the stencil is placed on the original design and fixed into place with adhesive tape. The design shows through the stencil as through a piece of tracing paper. Using a very sharp knife, cuts are made in the top layer of the stencil making sure that the backing material remains intact. The parts of the stencil representing the open or printing areas of the screen are peeled away from the backing material and the stencil transferred to the organdie, usually by ironing with a cool iron. Finally the backing material is removed leaving the stencil in place. On the whole, film stencils are expensive and I, personally, find the procedure rather mechanical. But there is no doubting their accuracy and reliability and for the production of such things as posters, where exact registration is required, film stencils are very useful.

Register

Registration (accurate overprinting) when producing multi-coloured prints, either by using the same screen several times or by using a number of screens in combination, is of vital importance. For much of the experimental work described so far it will be possible for the printer to locate the screen by eye, as in most instances there will be sufficient of the screen remaining unblocked to permit the original print to show through the organdie 'window', thereby ensuring that the new screen is in the correct position in relation to the colours already printed.

When using the same screen, slightly modified, for the second colour it is quite helpful to draw round the outside of the screen in pencil marking its position on each piece of printing paper. Provided that the screen does not have to be turned round, this line acts as an excellent guide.

When really accurate registration is required it becomes necessary to employ some kind of apparatus to locate the screen each time in an identical position in relation to the printing table. The traditional method of solving this problem is to hinge the back edge of the screen frame to a baseboard. The baseboard acts as the printing surface and has register marks against which the printing paper is located.

The screen can then be lowered into exactly the same position each time relying on the rigidity of the hinges to prevent lateral movement. In the case of a large screen, movement can be further guarded against by having a clip on the front edge of the screen frame which fastens to the baseboard. For commercial and other 'long run' printing, this type of apparatus work very well but it is not so convenient for the kind of work described in this book where, for example, the screen needs to be re-covered fairly frequently. It is possible however to obtain hinges with screw clamps which enable the operator to detach the screen from the baseboard more easily for re-covering.

The kind of apparatus shown on page 40 is simple to construct and does provide the printer with much more freedom to experiment.

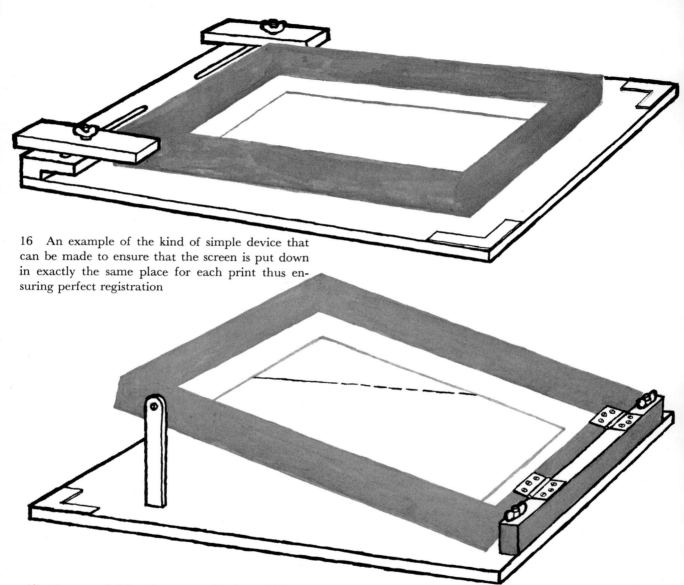

16 An example of the kind of simple device that can be made to ensure that the screen is put down in exactly the same place for each print thus ensuring perfect registration

17 A screen is hinged to a wooden bar which can in turn be bolted to a baseboard. The use of wing-nuts facilitates the removal of the screen and bar from the baseboard for re-covering. Small L-shaped pieces of card are glued or stapled to the corners of the baseboard into which the corners of the printing paper are located to ensure accurate registration

The production of textures

A texture is sometimes required as a component part of a design, either covering an area within the design, or as a background to which more work will be added later. Textured paper can also be fun to print as material for use in making paper collages. Incidentally it is a very good plan to keep all one's early experiments in screen printing, however unsuccessful they would seem to be, because they can be cut up to provide excellent material for collage pictures. A texture can be defined in this context as the variation of a surface. Paraffin wax provides, perhaps, some of the most interesting possibilities. In a liquid form wax can be dribbled, splattered or splashed on to the screen to produce interesting effects. The wax can also be used in a solid state to draw directly on to the organdie. If the screen is put down on a reasonable sympathetic surface, say two sheets of cartridge (drawing) paper on a smooth drawing board, it is possible to use the wax as a crayon, working the wax into the organdie and making sure that it fills the weave of the cotton and does not simply remain on the fibres. A screen can also be put down on an already textured surface, such as a piece of old and grainy timber, and a rubbing made. With any luck the texture of the surface being rubbed will transfer itself to the screen. Substances used in screen printing as in most other art and craft activities, can be put broadly into two catagories, i. e. those that mix with and are soluble in water (including emulsions of various kinds) and those that are oil or spirit based and require white spirit (mineral spirits), petrol (gasoline) or alcohol. This state of affairs can be exploited to produce a design on a screen, but obviously this can also present the beginner with some difficulties, and attention must be paid to the inherent nature of a material or substance before it is employed either as a blocking out agent or as a pigment. But the natural antipathy of oil and water can be equally well exploited in the production of texture effects. Paraffin wax together with gelatine or p.v.a. can be used in this way, and it is not difficult to devise texture producing techniques using other antipathetic substances. For example, rubber solution or rubber cement (petrol based) can be spread unevenly over the organdie, which can then be coated with gelatine and potassium dichromate. The rubber solution can be removed with petrol (or rubber cement thinner) leaving an open texture in its place. Wax rubbings can also be treated in this way to produce a positive result.

Producing screen photographically

By mixing potassium dichromate with gelatine a photo-sensitive substance is produced which can be made insoluble in water by exposure to light. As a result of this, all manner of possibilities are opened up for the production of screens by photographic means. Very little extra equipment is needed to make a screen photographically but one essential requirement is a light-tight cupboard, drawer or, if possible, a properly equipped darkroom in which the screens can be stored while they are drying. In its essentials the technique is as follows.

A screen is prepared with gelatine. When the gelatine is thoroughly dry it is very quickly coated with the potassium dichromate solution. Speed is an essential part of this operation as the gelatine will begin to harden as soon as the potassium dichromate dries. The length of time that the screen takes to dry completely will depend to a considerable extent on the warmth of the room but it will probably be at least 12 hours before every single part of the organdie is dry enough for the next process. All the time the screen is drying it must be kept in complete darkness. The design to be reproduced can be one of several different kinds but the basic requirement is that it should be executed in an opaque medium on a translucent background; black poster paint on tracing paper for example. Black indian ink is not generally opaque enough for this purpose. The design can be linear in character, but the ability to produce a very thin line depends to some extent on the quality of the material covering the screen. A drawing board or some similar board should be cut to fit exactly inside the screen (another good reason for standardising screen sizes) and should be supported on books, bricks or blocks of wood in such a way that the screen can be fitted on top, bottom up, without any part of the frame resting on the table. In other words the board must be pushed hard up against the inside organdie preventing any light from creeping in from below. The design should be fixed with transparent tape to a piece of glass; plate glass is best because of its weight, but heavy window glass will do. The design can now be sandwiched between the glass and the organdie of the screen, and the whole assemblage placed on the board and exposed to light, either in the light of a window or under a bright artifical light. The light will pass through the translucent parts of the design and harden the gelatine.

a

b

c

d

18 An exploded view of the arrangement for transferring a design to a screen photographically

a Glass with translucent design stuck to its underside by adhesive tape

b Screen prepared with gelatine and potassium dichromate

c Board cut to fit exactly inside the screen

d Support used to press the board hard up against the inside of the screen by keeping the screen frame off the table

Where the light is prevented from reaching the screen, by the black drawing, the gelatine will remain water soluble. The time taken by this process will vary with the light intensity, but by placing a coin or other opaque object on some unimportant part of the screen and moving it about from time to time, one can tell by the change in colour of the organdie from yellow to brown that the hardening process has taken place. As a very rough guide this process should take about half an hour in fairly direct daylight. The screen must now be moved away quickly and washed in warm water, preferably under the pressure of a hot water tap. The unexposed areas of gelatine will be washed away leaving an open screen in their place, which will print as an exact replica of the original design. Care must be taken when positioning the design on the organdie to ensure that the design is transferred on to the screen the correct way round so that it does not print as a mirror image of the original.

This photographic technique is capable of infinite refinement. The most detailed intricate work is possible using camera produced photographic negatives and very fine silk but this kind of work is, in my view, better left until one has had considerable screen printing experience. However, a great deal of satisfaction can be derived from making screens photographically from prints, and rubbings from natural objects, achieving the kind of results that would not be possible by any other method.

Fabric printing

Screen printing is a technique by means of which an image can be created and repeated. In that sense it is simply an instrument of reproduction, and it is with this basic aspect of the subject that this book is concerned. Nevertheless the procedures for producing the image on the screen are the same whether the screen is to be used for prints, posters or lengths of fabric, and I am sure that many readers will want to try their hand at printing on cloth experimentally, particularly as some of the dyes used in these early experiments for print making are really designed for use on fabric. For a simple experiment in this field I would suggest that a screen be prepared with an exactly square 'window'. This can be filled with a design, using any of the techniques already discussed, which radiates from the centre so that when the screen is printed on the same square of material four times, each time turning the screen through an angle of 90°, a very rich overprinted pattern will result. If a Helizarin dye is used, the process is exactly the same as that used for printing on paper, with two modifiications. Firstly a little *Condensol* is added to the dye mixture just before printing (read manufacturer's instructions). Secondly after printing, the fabric should be heated to 100° C for one hour, to fix the dye. In practice this means slowly ironing the material on both sides with a hot flat iron.

The printed squares can be used to make such things as scatter cushions and scarf squares. It is also possible to produce a number of similar, though not identical, squares which can be joined together to make a decorative hanging. This is a very good way of bringing together the work of pupils or students in a screen printing class. Any decorative hanging of this kind can be further developed using machine or hand embroidery; the original screen print acting as a starting point for an adventure into another decorative craft. An open screen is also useful as a way of applying dye to material in wax resist work (batik). Squares of cotton can be prepared with batik wax, and the dye applied by squeegee through an open screen. Of course here size is limited by the size of the screen, but this is not usually a problem in a teaching situation where one is generally only working on a relatively small scale.

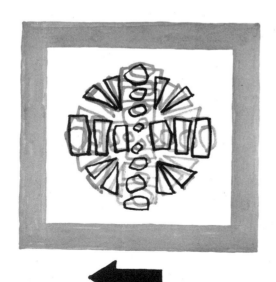

19 Printing and turning a square screen through 90° to build up an overprinted design

Posters

Screen printing is widely used in the world of commercial art, printing and packaging, to reproduce both illustrative material and lettering. The commercial screen printer quite often works with only basic equipment. He is naturally interested in speed and mass-production and any modification of the basic process described in this book is generally concerned with this aspect of the subject. For example, the squeegee is held by movable metal arms which have an attachment to counterbalance the weight of the squeegee. Also the paper is often held in place on the printing surface by vacuum pressure. In the case of the small back street printer, these refinements, if they exist at all, are often very crude and home-made and the quality and precision of the work produced under these conditions is quite remarkable.

Almost any of the techniques so far described can be used to put lettering on a screen; the choice of technique will depend on the scale of the lettering required. For example, it would not be practical to attempt small lettering using wax, nor would wax be suitable as a medium if a large number of prints were needed, as the wax would tend to break down before the end of the run. On the other hand, for a bold effect to be produced quickly, or for a background wax would be ideal. Probably the most suitable technique for most purposes is the one using gelatine, lacquer and potassium dichromate.

The recent development of a wide range of 'instant lettering' (self-adhesive plastic lettering, e. g. *Letraset*) sold in sheets has been a great boon to the screen printer. Using this material a poster can be created on tracing paper or transparent plastic film and transferred to the screen photographically.

It is also possible to use instant lettering, instead of lacquer, to protect a gelatine screen from potassium dichromate. It is even possible to use the plastic letters to block out the screen directly by rubbing them down on to the organdie and then fixing them in place with the aerosol fixative supplied by the manufacturer. The fixative must be used sparingly as it is in itself a form of lacquer and could block the screen. It is important to remember, when using all these techniques, to work on the inside of the screen otherwise the lettering will appear the wrong way round.

The kind of organdie I have recommended for most of the experiments in this book will not be fine enough for very small lettering. For letters of less than about $^3/_8$ in. in height it would be advisable to cover the screen with fine silk.

A screen can be used as a very crude form of duplicator to produce quick posters or notices. If a drawing is made on a plain organdie with a soft graphic pencil, this can be transferred to paper by simply squeegeeing plain Helizarin binder across it. Several prints can be made in this way until the graphite is exhausted.

Posters and the teacher

Any teacher who has ever introduced a printmaking technique into a school will be familiar with the inherent dangers of such an action. The head teacher immediately assumes that henceforth all his printing problems will be solved quickly and cheaply by printing everything from the school stationery to the school magazine on the school premises. Soon other members of the staff catch the fever and sports day numbers, carol concert programmes and open day notices are added to the list. If an art teacher tries to explain that asking his children to cope with all this is rather like suggesting to the sports teacher that his first team be entered for a national tournament, he is regarded as failing in his job.

Obviously screen printing, like any other form of printing in a school situation, should be regarded as an educational activity for the benefit of the children. Project work, which may include a certain amount of poster making, can of course be a valuable part of an education programme, and it is here that screen printing can prove to be a very useful medium.

I have indicated a range of possibilities by reproducing two film society posters (80–84) both of which are intended to be put on a display board with the detailed information relating to a particular film programme or activity written in by hand. The first is simply a direct painting on to the screen in paraffin wax. The second illustrates the use of the more sophisticated photographic techniques.

General hints

Do's and don'ts that may be helpful in the early stages.

Never try to print with a wet screen, i. e. a screen that has just been washed out with water; the results will be disastrous whatever the medium used for printing. If it is necessary to change the colour and continue printing immediately, wipe the screen out with a barely-damp sponge.

Do not be discouraged if the first print from any screen is smudgy. A screen often needs to be 'run-in' on scrap paper before the printing proper begins.

Some plastic cartons and synthetic sponges dissolve in spirit or alcohol. It is therefore advisable to check this factor before using items made of plastic with substances containing either of these liquids.

Remember that an open screen will use more pigment than a heavily blocked one. Always ensure that there is sufficient pigment in a screen before making the print.

Never leave a screen standing idle with pigment in it for more than a few minutes.

Never try to print a screen on to which some unwanted pigment has fallen. If this should happen during printing always clear the screen before proceeding by placing it on a sheet of newspaper and squeegeeing the unwanted pigment away.

Covered screens are fragile. Never leave a screen where it will be blown down by the draught if someone opens the door, or on the floor where a foot can easily be put through it.

Be patient. Never try to print a screen until the blocking out material is thoroughly dry.

Always take enough prints of a screen in its first state before altering. It is surprising how many prints get used up during experimental work.

Always keep plenty of clean rag handy for emergencies.

Summary of experiments

For easy reference the following are summaries of the processes already described. Whenever possible I have suggested cheap and readily obtainable materials which can be used quite as successfully as those obtained from the screen printing supplier. My object in doing this is not only to make screen printing as economical as possible for the beginner but also to impress on him the experimental nature of the craft. Screen printing is not a closed, traditional craft with set methods and procedures. 'If it works use it' has always been my approach to the subject and because of the simple principle underlying the technique this policy has generally succeeded.

These experiments start from the point where a screen or screens have been covered with organdie and where a printing surface in the form of a screen printing table or newspaper pad has been prepared.

'Negative' methods

1 *Materials*

Gumstrip (brown paper tape)
Newsprint
Pigment in the form of water based paint or dye
Printing paper

Method

Mask the surround of the screen with gumstrip, arrange newsprint shapes on the printing paper, place the screen on the newsprint shapes and squeegee pigment across the screen picking up shapes, turn the screen round on itself and print again. Continue printing after changing the colour and rearranging or changing the shapes.

2 *Materials*
Gumstrip (brown paper tape)
Pigment in the form of water based paint or dye
Printing paper

Method
Mask the surround of the screen with gumstrip, cut gumstrip shapes and stick them to the underside of the screen to form a design. Make several prints and then wipe the screen clean, add new gumstrip shapes to those already in position and print again on top of the first prints using either the same or a second colour, repeat until a satisfactory result is obtained.

3 *Materials*
Gumstrip (brown paper tape)
Pigment in the form of water based paint or dye
Printing paper
Paraffin wax melted in a can inside a saucepan of water or in a glue pot
Old hog-hair or bristle paint brush

Method
Turn screen bottom side up and paint design on to organdie in the molten wax making sure that the wax is always liquid by constantly dipping the brush back into the hot wax.
Print the screen and add more wax and print again until a satisfactory print has been produced.
Wax can be removed completely or in part with a hot iron between sheets of newspaper.

4 *Materials*
Gumstrip (brown paper tape)
Pigment (spirit based ink)
Animal glue (scotch glue prepared in a glue pot) or gum
Printing paper
Strip of thick card about 2 inches wide

Method
With the screen bottom side up create a design on the organdie with the glue using the cardboard strip as a spreader. It is also possible to produce lines of glue using the edge of the strip of card.
Print as before.

5 *Materials*

Gumstrip (brown paper tape)

Pigment (water or spirit soluble)

Lacquer (screen lacquer or ordinary lacquer purchased from a hardware store)

Printing paper

Soft hair brush (an old sable brush or something similar, size about No 3)

Method

This experiment demonstrates a method for producing a fine linear design. Paint the design directly on to the underside of the organdie in lacquer, allow to dry and print.

There are many other substances with which to experiment and which will satisfactorily block out the screen, for example, white *Shellac* dissolved in methylated spirit or alcohol (or button polish), plastic emulsion paint, asphaltum. Some of these substances remain soluble when dry, and can easily be removed. Others are difficult, if not impossible, to shift should any correction to the design be necessary.

All substances, when used as described in methods 1 to 5, will produce a negative, i. e. a white design on a coloured background. The following experiments demonstrate methods of producing a positive design, i. e. a coloured design on a white or plain coloured background. Experiments 6, 7 and 8 are extensions or adaptions of 3, 4 and 5.

'Positive' methods

6 *Materials*

Pigment (water or spirit soluble)
Paraffin wax
Old hog-hair or bristle brush
Either polyvinyl acetate, (p.v.a.) or white glue, plastic emulsion or acrylic
   paint or gelatine and potassium dichromate (prepared as suggested on
   page 58)
1½ in. (approx.) paint or varnish brush

Method

Prepare a design as in 3, using molten wax. When the wax has set the screen
should be coated with one of the liquid substances listed above, using a paint
or varnish brush. If care is taken to ensure that the coating substance is painted well up the sides of the screen there will be no need to mask out with
gumstrip, although this can be done if 'leaks' appear during the printing.
When the coating substance is thoroughly dry, the screen should be held up
to the light to see that no pin holes of unfilled organdie are visible. Should
there be the slightest sign suggesting that the organdie has not been filled
another application of coating medium is necessary. When finally satisfied
that the screen is completely blocked the wax can be removed either by washing in hot water or by ironing with a warm iron between sheets of newspaper.
When using p.v.a. (white glue) or emulsion paint (acrylic) the washing
technique is preferable. When the wax has been removed and the screen
allowed to dry printing can proceed in the usual way. The print should exactly
reproduce the original wax painting.

7 *Materials*

Pigment
Glue
Black waterproofing compound (asphaltum)
White spirit (mineral spirits) or petrol (gasoline)
1½ in. paint or varnish brush
Old hog-hair or bristle paint brush

Method

The design should be painted on to the organdie with the black compound using the hog-hair or bristle brush. It may be necessary to reduce the compound with a little white spirit (mineral spirits) or petrol (gasoline) if it is too stiff to use in its original state. But care should be taken not to thin it to the point where it loses its 'body'. Next the screen is coated with glue and this is allowed to dry. The compound is then removed with white spirit or petrol which will not affect the water soluble glue. The screen can be printed in the usual way preferably using spirit soluble screen printing inks.

8 *Materials*

Pigment (water or spirit soluble)
Gelatine
Potassium dichromate
Lacquer
Large soft brush as described in the text for applying the gelatine
Fine lacquer brush as in 5

Method

Coat the screen with gelatine (see page 37). When this is thoroughly dry, paint the design on to the gelatine with lacquer. When the lacquer is dry a wash of potassium dichromate solution is applied over all. This is allowed to dry and the screen is then set in a light place for the gelatine and dichromate to react, i. e. turn from orange to brown. The screen is then washed in hot water dissolving the gelatine lying under the lacquer which comes away leaving an open screen in its place. Print when dry.

9 *Materials*

Pigment (water or spirit based)
Gelatine
Potassium dichromate
Large soft brush
Black poster paint or thick powder paint
Thin drawing paper or tracing paper
Printing paper
Thin lubricating oil
Fine brushes

Method

Coat the screen with gelatine and allow to dry. Working quickly apply wash of potassium dichromate. Place screen in light-tight box, drawer or darkroom to dry—this may take several hours during which time no light must be allowed to reach the screen. The design to be reproduced should be prepared on thin drawing or tracing paper, using poster or other thick paint. If drawing paper is used it must be made translucent by oiling the back with lubricating oil. After blotting off surplus oil, the design can then be brought into contact with the screen and exposed to light. Wash out unfixed gelatine, allow the screen to dry and print.

These nine experiments do not summarise all the ground covered in the main text but should provide a sufficiently comprehensive basic experience to give the beginner confidence in handling the medium.

Substances used in screen printing

Many readers will have had experience of the substances mentioned in this book in other contexts, but for quick reference I have drawn out the table of properties printed below. In very general, and rather unscientific terms, most of the substances used in screen printing can be classified under one of three headings according to the solvents used in their preparation and use, namely (1) water based; (2) spirit based, e. g. white spirit (mineral spirits), turpentine, or petrol (gasoline); (3) alcohol based (methylated spirits). Some substances remain soluble in the original solvent when dry, some require a different solvent at that stage and others become virtually insoluble. It is of the utmost importance to know the nature of the substances being used as either blocking out agents, or as printing media. In this way disasters, such as removing the blocking out material with the printing medium, can be avoided and the printer will also be in a better position to exploit the properties of these substances in obtaining interesting effects. I repeat, there are very many substances that can be used or adapted for use in the various aspects of screen printing, many of which have not been fully dealt with in this book. There are many proprietary products, of fairly recent invention, which it would be impossible to include in the table below, but this should not prevent the reader from experimenting with them if he thinks they will satisfy a particular requirement.

Substance	Mixed with or soluble in	Soluble when dry in	Brushes, screens cleaned in	Points to note
Gelatine	Warm water (not boiling)	Warm water	Warm water	Insoluble when mixed with potassium dichromate and exposed to light
Glue (scotch or hide)	Hot water	Hot water	Hot water	

Substance	Mixed with or soluble in	Soluble when dry in	Brushes, screens cleaned in	Points to note
Gum (arabic tragacanth British)	Warm water	Warm water	Warm water	
Polyvinyl acetate	Water	Alcohol (methylated spirit)	Alcohol	Brushes etc can be washed in water if p.v.a. has not been allowed to dry
Plastic emulsion paint (acrylic)	Water	Alcohol	Alcohol	
Shellac (white or button polish)	Alcohol	Alcohol	Alcohol	
Paraffin wax	Usually melted without solvent	White spirit (mineral spirits) turpentine or petrol (gasoline)	White spirit (mineral spirits)	Paraffin can be added to liquid wax to aid flow
Lacquer (oil)	White spirit (mineral spirits)	Not easily	White spirit (mineral spirits)	When hard can be removed with paint stripper
Lacquer (cellulose)	Special thinner	Not easily	Special thinner	As above
Asphaltum (black water-proofing compound)	White spirit or petrol (gasoline)	White spirit or petrol (gasoline)	White spirit or petrol (gasoline)	

Recipes

Included below is a quick reference table of basic recipes. The quantities given in most of these recipes are approximate and can be varied to produce a stronger or weaker substance as experience requires.

Glue, glue size
1-2 heaped tablespoonfuls of granulated or powdered glue to ½ pint water.
Mix the glue into the water and heat in a water jacket until completely dissolved. Do not boil and do not stir too briskly.
Glue in sheet or cake form should be treated in the same way but should be broken up and allowed to stand in the water overnight if possible. Use warm. Storage time when mixed is limited unless a few drops of antiseptic are added.
Proprietary or branded glues
Use according to manufacturer's directions.

Gum
When in lump or powdered form gum should be prepared in the same manner as described above. Use warm or cold. Store in airtight jar.

Proprietary or branded gums
These are supplied prepared ready for use and can generally be thinned with water if necessary.

Gelatine (photographic)
2 heaped tablespoonfuls of granulated gelatine to ½ pint water.
Prepare in the same way as glue. DO NOT BOIL. Use whilst warm but when cold should set to a stiff jelly. Can be re-heated but do not try to store for more than a few days. The addition of a level teaspoon of potassium dichromate produces a photo-sensitive substance which when dry and exposed to light becomes insoluble in water.

Polyvinal acetate (p.v.a.) or white glue
Use as supplied by manufacturer either in the form of adhesive or as medium for powder tempera colours. Can be thinned with water if necessary.

'Green' screen filler
Use as supplied. Do not thin.

Polycell (wallpaper paste) and dye
(domestic dye powder)
Make up a small quantity of Polycell (or a comparable wallpaper paste) in the manner suggested by the manufacturer but using rather less water. Dissolve the domestic dye powder in, say, ¼ pint of warm water and stir into the prepared Polycell. Quantities must be adjusted to fit the type and amount of printing to be done.

Starch paste and dye
Can be prepared and used very much in the manner described above.

Helizarin fabric dye or Acco-Lite
For printmaking on paper simply add pigment to binder 'D' until desired colour is achieved. All colours are intermixable but some, black for example, are much stronger than others so that care must be taken when mixing. On average about one tablespoon of pigment will give a good colour to about ¾ pint of binder. Binder 'R' can be added to reduce the mixture. For printing on fabric follow manufacturer's directions.

Oil bound screen inks
To produce prints with matt opaque surface use as supplied by manufacturer after thinning with a little white spirit (mineral spirits).
To produce transparent prints with overprinting effects add ink to transparent medium in the proportion of approximately one of ink to two of medium. Thin with white spirit (mineral spirits) as before.

Shellac

Flake shellac should be just covered with methylated spirits (alcohol) in a sealed jar and allowed to stand for several hours until the shellac has dissolved. The solution can then be further thinned with methylated spirits until a usable consistency is achieved. A ready prepared shellac can be purchased under one of the following names from hardware stores: White shellac, french polish, button polish or patent knotting.

Lacquer (oil bound)

Use as supplied. Can be thinned with white spirit (mineral spirits) but should not be over-thinned as this will cause it to spread on the screen.

Black waterproofing compound
(asphaltum)

There are many varieties of this substance produced for use in the building trade. Some are rather thick and require to be thinned with white spirit (mineral spirits).

Paraffin wax

Crumble solid wax into container in a water jacket and heat until liquid. Do not heat directly, particularly over an open flame, as highly inflammable vapour will be given off. Paraffin oil can be added to prevent the wax from setting too quickly whilst it is being applied but this will weaken the final film. It is preferable to use the wax very hot.

Cellulose lacquer

Use as supplied. Do not thin. Requires special solvent (as supplied by the manufacturer).

Examples of techniques

The illustrations from pages 62–89 do not necessarily coincide with the summaries of experiments on pages 50–55. In the majority of cases two or more techniques are combined to produce each print. The captions however do give a clear indication of the methods employed in each example and it is hoped that the reader will be able to refer to these illustrations when planning his own work.

1 Paraffin wax has been used to block the screen which has
been printed and turned round on itself and printed again

2 A print made by picking up newsprint shapes. The same screen has been turned round on itself and printed using the same dye

3 Glue has been used to block out the screen and after a number of prints have been made in a pale colour further work has been added, again using glue. The modified screen has then been used to add a second colour. It must be remembered that with a 'negative' screen additional work on the screen increases the white or unprinted area

4   Rectangular gumstrip shapes stuck to underside of screen. More added for the
second print. Third print made by turning the screen round on itself in the
final state

5 A 'pick-up' screen using cut newspaper shapes which were removed after the first colour had been printed and replaced by new shapes that had been cut and arranged on one of the original prints

6 A lacquer screen worked on progressively, adding more lacquer after the
printing of each colour

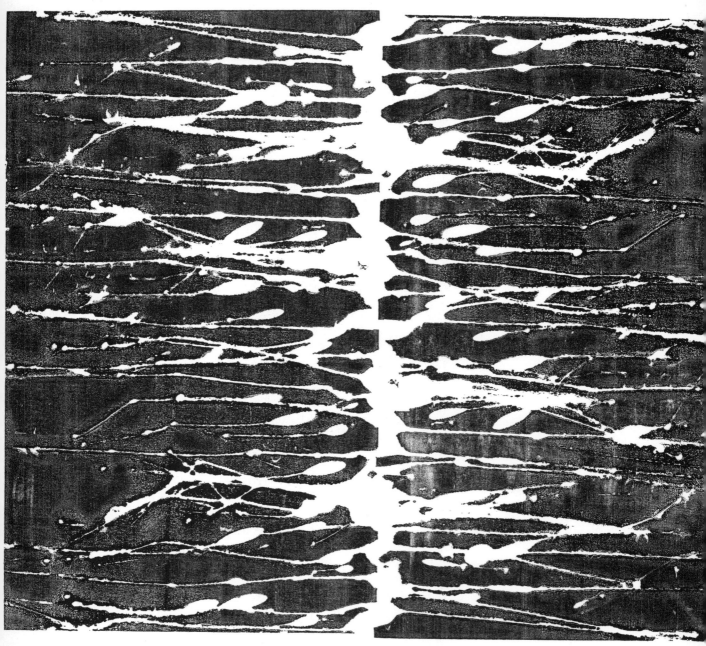

70

8 A piece of solid paraffin wax was used to make rubbings of various textured surfaces directly on to the organdie. The screen was then coated with gelatine and potassium dichromate, was allowed to dry and harden and the wax removed with a warm iron

Opposite

7 A texture print produced by splashing molten paraffin wax along the top edge of a screen held almost vertical, allowing the wax to dribble down. Quite an interesting effect is produced when the screen is turned and prints are made side by side

ABC *lacquer*

10 A screen coated on the inside with gelatine was prote
from potassium dichromate by screen lacquer and ins
lettering. Screen lacquer was used to paint in the v
'lacquer' after the screen had been washed out and d

9 A 'negative' screen produced by painting directly in glue
on to the organdie

72

texture produced by applying gum to a screen with a sponge

12 A texture produced by dribbling 'green' screen filler on to the screen and spreading it with a piece of card

13 A 'negative' wax screen, mainly painted direct in molten wax but including some rubbing with solid wax (a) was made 'positive' by coating with gelatine and potassium dichromate and removing the wax (b). A supplementary screen was prepared in shellac and superimposed in a second colour on the positive print

14 (a) Cut paper
  (b) Cut paper

15 (a) Wax
(b) Cut paper

Prints produced by students on an experimental one day course

16 Prints were made from a cut paper 'pick-up' screen (a). The paper shapes were removed and the screen cleaned. Wax rubbings from grainy timber were made directly on to the organdie in the spaces where the paper shapes had been. The side areas of the screen were filled with molten wax and the screen used to print a second colour

17 A film society poster produced by simply painting directly on to the screen in molten wax. The space has been left for the insertion of detailed information at the time when the poster is needed

18 The stages in making a screen from an ordinary photograph

a Part of the original photograph of a scene on Broadway

b This is transformed into a 'Kodalith' print by projecting the negative on to Kodalith translucent printing paper. This process requires the use of a darkroom and Kodalith paper and developer (see list of suppliers) but is no more difficult to handle than normal enlarging and processing. The effect is to produce a positive print in which all the intermediate tones have been resolved to either black or white

c The Kodalith print is put in contact with a gelatine and potassium dichromate prepared screen and treated as described on page 42. The final result is a very much simplified version of the original. The success of such a process depends very largely on the choice of the original photograph but if a reasonably contrasted original is used the results are often quite exciting

19   A film society poster using the photographically produced screen described on page 81. The background consisted of an open screen on to the inside of which the words 'film society' were fixed in instant lettering. Un-treated lettering stands up to a reasonable amount of careful printing but if possible it should be sprayed with the specially provided aerosol fixative which has the effect of binding the lettering very firmly into the organdie. Care must be taken not to hold the nozzle of the spray too close to the organdie or the screen may become blocked

20 Another use for the photographically produced screen. In this instance the screen was printed with a paper strip across the middle which produced a white area which was later filled by another screen containing the wording, again using instant lettering

21 Yet another variation of the film society notice, this time using a screen made photographically from an antique printer's 'fist'

film society

film society

22   A texture print made by allowing rubber solution to run across the screen and dry. The screen was then coated with glue and the rubber solution removed with petrol. The glue has broken down slightly giving the finer texture

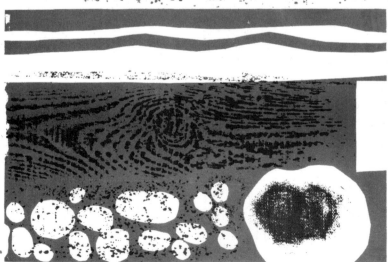

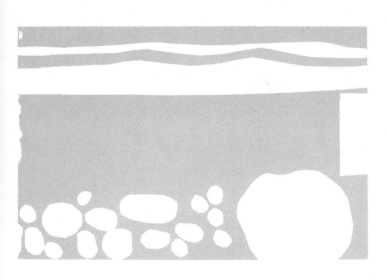

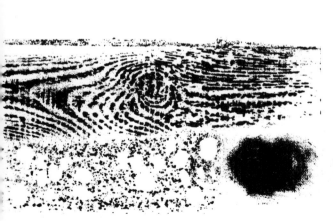

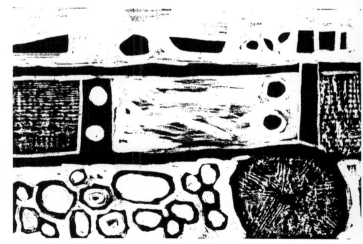

23   A combination of wax, including wax rubbing, and paper 'pick-up'

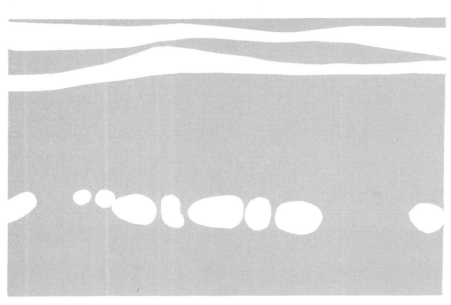

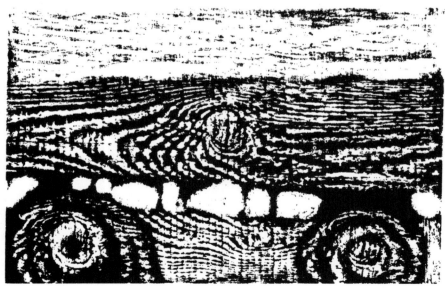

24　A variation on 23. In this case a film stencil was used to
produce the final screen including the boat shapes

a

b(i)

b(ii)

c(i)

c(ii)

25 A three screen print using (a) wax rubbing (b) wax rubbing and some wax painting and (c) wax painting made positive with a coating of gelatine and potassium dichromate

26   Prints by an experienced desi[...]
     using simple techniques

     (a) 3 screen print using glue[...]

     (b) 4 screen print using glue[...]

     (c) 3 screen print using glue[...]

Suppliers in Great Britain

Specialist screen printing equipment and materials including inks
Davis (Patents) Ltd
   18 Phipp Street, London E C 2
Selectasine Silk Screens Ltd
   22 Bulstrode Street, London W 1
Screen Process Supplies Ltd
   24 Parsons Green Lane, London S W 6
T N Lawrence & Son Ltd
   2 Bleeding Heart Yard, Greville Street
   London E C 1

Screen equipment and general art and handicraft supplies
Dryad Handicrafts Ltd
   Northgates, Leicester and 22 Bloomsbury Street
   London W C 1

Dyestuffs
Helizarin
   Skilbeck Bros. Ltd
   55-57 Glengall Road, London S E 15
Tinolite
   Geigy (UK) Limited
   42 Berkeley Square, London W 1
   and Simonsway, Manchester 22
Procion (in small quantities)
   Mayborn Products Ltd
   139-147 Sydenham Road, London S E 26
   For large quantities enquiries should be
   directed to the nearest Imperial Chemical
   Industries' sales office

Adhesives
   P.V.A. (Marvin Medium)
   Margros Ltd
   Monument Way, West Woking, Surrey

Photographic equipment
   Kodak Limited
   246 High Holborn
   London W C 1 and branches

Suppliers in the USA

Screen process colors and equipment
Graphic Arts Center
 1534 W. Seventh Street
 Los Angeles, California

Screen Process Supply Mfg Co.
 1199 E. 12th Street
 Oakland, California

Arts & Crafts Colony
 42nd & North Tamiami Trail
 Sarasota, Florida

Jordan Equipment Company
 1101 13th Street
 Colombus, Georgia

Atlas Silk Screen Supply
 1733 Milwaukee Avenue
 Chicago, Illinois

Chicago Silk Screen Supply
 882 Milwaukee Avenue
 Chicago, Illinois

Process Supply Company
 313 Hanley Industrial Park
 St. Louis, Missouri

Standard Screen Supply Corp.
 54 West 21st Street
 New York, N. Y.

Active Process Supply Co.
 457 West Broadway
 New York, N. Y.

Silk Screen Supplies Inc.
 33 Lafayette Avenue
 Brooklyn, New York

Dyestuffs
Acco-Lite colors
American Crayon Company
 Sandusky, Ohio
Procion (minimum 1 lb)
Chemical Manufacturing Company
 Madison Avenue, New York, N. Y.

Rubber roller
Rapid Roller Company Limited
 2556 S. Federal Street, Chicago 16

Shellac
Acme Shellac Products Company
 104 Blanchard Street
 Newark, New Jersey

Bibliography

Textile Printing and Dyeing   Nora Proud, *Batsford London, and Reinhold New York*

Creative Print Making *(British edition)*   Peter Green, *Batsford London*

New Creative Print Making *(U.S. edition)*   Peter Green, *Watson-Guptill New York*

Print Making With a Spoon   Norman Gorbaty, *Reinhold New York*

Printmaking Without a Press   Janet Erickson and Adelaide Sproul, *Reinhold New York*

Linocuts and Woodcuts   Michael Rothenstein, *Studio Vista London*

Print Your Own Fabrics   Jutta Lammer, *Batsford London, and Watson-Guptill New York*

Simple Printmaking   Cyril Kent and Mary Cooper, *Studio Vista London, and Watson-Guptill New York*

Surface Printing   Peter Green, *Batsford London, and Watson-Guptill New York*

Creative Textile Craft: Thread and Fabric   Rolf Hartung, *Batsford London, and Reinhold New York*

Colour and Texture in Creative Textile Craft   Rolf Hartung, *Batsford London, and Reinhold New York*

Printed Rag Toys   Joy Wilcox, *Batsford London*